# Correcting Corrections

*A Look at the Insanity of an
Institution That Cultivates and
Unleashes More Violent* and *Adept
Criminals Back Into Our Cities*

by Rick Saldan

**Motivational Magic
Publications**

*ALSO BY RICK SALDAN*

*Super Learning: How to Get Straight A's*

*Breaking Free of the Matrix*

*Spiritual Influences on Classic Literature*

*Cold War Essays on Societal Breakdown*

*Lupus, How to Survive and Thrive*

*Kennedy Death Squads*

*Confronting Racial Hatred With Classic Literature*

*Using Theatrical Stage Magic to
Assess Cognitive Development*

*Excelling With Excel*

Rick Saldan's Motivational Magic
www.MotivationalMagic.com
Copyright © 2017-2020, Rick Saldan
All rights reserved.
ISBN: 1974267601
ISBN-13: 978-1974267606

# Two Free eBooks

Your support is greatly appreciated! To thank you for your interest in this topic and for buying my books, here are two free ebooks that I thought you might enjoy!

## DEDICATION

This book is dedicated to the corrections officers, sheriffs, police officers, judges, attorneys, prosecutors, public defenders, social workers, social activists, and all the dedicated diligent workers that make up our overall criminal justice system.

This book is also dedicated to the many that have served their sentences, and are determined to make a good life for themselves; to never return to a correctional facility ever again. I have the deepest respect for such individuals and all that you have had to overcome.

The time has come to revamp this antiquated dysfunctional system that continues to create, develop and release thousands of dangerous and violent criminals back into society. Let's stop paying for an expensive system that makes bad people even worse.

# CONTENTS

CHAPTER ONE

*The Insanity of Needlessly Tolerating Gross Failure*

I have been the victim of violent crime several times: while attending Central High School, while attending Temple University, while walking the streets near Philadelphia's City Hall, while riding the subway, and while attending a concert.

When you are accosted and injured in such a manner, it eats away at you for many months. It is upsetting to realize that such people will go on continuing to hurt others. Some do it for thrills. Some do it because they enjoy hurting others. Some do it because they are broke and need money.

Picture this. Imagine you have a big swimming pool in your backyard. Your friends come over frequently for your festive parties and barbeques. After a few months, you notice the water is turning green and some of your friends have been getting sick. The pool man tells you that the filtration system is too small, and you invest in a bigger filtration unit. Instead of cleaning the water, it only spews out more dirt and toxins into the water. More and more people are getting sick. Again, you purchase an even larger filtration system. But it simply spews out more dirt and toxins into the water. The very system you invested in to clean your water and keep your friends healthy is the system that is instead spewing out dirt and toxins that are hurting people you love.

Pardon some of the unintentional harsh realities of that metaphor, but this is exactly what is happening to cities all over America. The very system we have implemented to reduce crime and make us safe is instead spewing out people who are angrier, more violent and better skilled at crime. Do you see the insanity of this system?

We all heard the quote that insanity is doing the same thing over and over again and expecting different results. While that quote is commonly attributed to Albert Einstein, there is not any evidence of that in his writings. Nevertheless, this quote can aptly fit the lack of success with the American corrections system.

All of us pay such heavy costs for tolerating a failing corrections system. We all loathe the horrible crime statistics in our country. We despise the very thought of raising children in such a violent society. We know that the recidivism rates of prisons are incredibly high, and that we send these men and women back into our cities more violent, more skillful, and more predatory in their crimes. A small fraction successfully reintegrates into society and vows to never return to the justice system, but not enough.

Why do we continue to tolerate this madness? Why do we have an institutional structure in place that clearly does the exact opposite of what it has been put there to do? I am not looking to point fault at those who work in the corrections system. They are doing the jobs they were hired to do, just as they were trained to do. I am finding fault with those we elect to govern our cities, and those we entrust to bring improvement to the world we live in today.

If I were to come running over to you and hand you an all-expenses paid vacation to any destination of your choice, would you accept the airline ticket? Most likely. What if you found out that the airline the ticket was purchased from only had a success rate of 30%, would you accept the ticket then? Most likely not!

For many such industries, such an abysmal success ratio would be completely unacceptable. This holds true for countless endeavors of industry, such as automobile manufacturing, medical hospitals, hospitality, and countless others. If any such vendors were publicly exposed as having such an atrocious track record, word would get out as quick as wildfire and that proprietor would soon find himself out of business and in the unemployment line.

## CHAPTER TWO

## Astounding Administrative Costs and Wasted Tax Dollars

Sadly, this has been the undeniable case for our institution of corrections for countless decades, and very little has been done to rectify the situation. The United States Department of Justice indicates that our nation spends more than $70 billion every year on corrections and prisons. Our country spends another $40 billion per year on its judicial system, and an additional $100 billion on police and law enforcement personnel.[1] A combined investment of $210 billion is spent every year, largely due to the fact that we have grown blind and woefully tolerant of a mammoth corrections system that simply does not work.

Think of the awesome transformation our country would enjoy if we were to take a fraction of that $210 billion and invest it more wisely into other critical areas of infrastructure that are in dire need of the infusion of cash, such as higher quality public education to reduce the illiteracy rate among poorer neighborhoods, medical care for the 80 million who cannot afford it, free college tuition for anyone who wanted to enroll, business ownership training to reduce the 40% poverty level, and so on. We have countless social needs in our country that are being ignored as vast sums of money are spent elsewhere in places around the world that never impact us.

Not only are we harboring malfunctioning machinery that is bleeding our economy dry, but the costs of this corrections machinery have been sharply escalating for the last forty years. On the municipal level, expenditures on the criminal justice system have gone up 422% since 1982. On the state level, we have seen increases of 548% since that same year. On the federal level, our Department of Corrections has exploded like the Tasmanian devil with budget cost increases of 749%.

The national average for recidivism, meaning those who are released from prison winding back up in prison within five to ten years, is at 77% within five years and 83% within ten years. These statistics start dropping the older the offender is. For those that are rearrested within five years, 84.1% of those were under age 24; 78.6% of those rearrested were ages 25 through 39; and, 69.2% of those rearrested were age 40 or older. [2]

Among various types of crimes, there were definitely several types of crimes were the rates of recidivism were considerably higher than most other types of crime. Among those with higher recidivism rate include robbery (70.2%), burglary (74.0%), larceny (74.6%), car theft (78.8%), possessing or selling stolen property (77.4%) and trafficking in illegal weapons (70.2%).

These various statistics hold relatively true throughout various levels of government, to include municipal, state and federal detention facilities. This shocking statistic was compiled by painstakingly following the lives of one-third of our national prison population. For those who were released from correctional facilities, they were monitored for up to ten years.

If those individuals were again incarcerated within a time period of three years, they were added to the list being compiled by this federal study on recidivism. Note, please, that this particular timeline was only three years. This suggests that for those inmates who wound up being arrested after four or five years, the recidivism rate across the United States would actually be much higher. Berlatsky addresses the question of whether mere punishment serves effectively as a deterrent.

"The high levels of repeat offending among those who have [already] served a prison sentence suggest that imprisonment does not act as an effective form of deterring individuals from crime, although we cannot calculate how many crimes are avoided because potential criminals are deterred by the prospect of imprisonment".[3]

The impact of the monumental failure on a national scale impacts every single one of us each and every day. We see its impact in every facet of our day to day lives. We live in fear when walking the streets of some neighborhoods, as well as always being on the alert for the safety and security of our homes and our families. Our economy is impacted both by the financial losses incurred by highly skilled criminals, as well as the requirement for constantly hiring more law enforcement officers.

Our insurance rates are higher due to exorbitant rates of insurance fraud conducted by highly educated criminals. It can be argued that there is not a single facet of our daily lives that is not somehow impacted by the trickle down effects of each of us living in a crime-ridden society.

In his book *Kiss of Death: America's Love Affair with the Death Penalty*, author John Bessler brings forward many examples of the endlessly outward ripples that even a single crime introduces into the lives of law abiding citizens, both to the victims of that crime, and to the family and friends surrounding that person. Even a small crime such as a burglary can have long-term impact in robbing people of their sense of security and well-being. The emotional impact and subsequent personal difficulties can last several months, impacting professional performance at work, at college, and relationships within marriages, family life and social ties. As Bessler says, "criminal acts, whether committed in New York or in our own neighborhoods, have a profound impact on American life".[4]

CHAPTER   THREE

### *Prisons Are Schools Teaching Excellence in Criminal Endeavors*

The high percentage of convicted and released criminals living among us is quite shocking once you start digging into the numbers. In the zip code where I live, there are 44 sex offenders living right here among us, with another 63 living in the bigger township nearby. The corrections system in our country is basically a revolving door, where a convicted felon is warehoused for a set time period.

They serve their time, with very few rehabilitative processes in place which make any concerted effort to turn the lives of those inmates around and set their feet upon the proper path. As Berlatsky states in his book "Imprisonment",

"Prisons must be places where a person is sent for the purpose of rehabilitation into society. Our prisons must be places where attitudes are corrected. They must be structures which prevent further crime, rather than simply holding prisoners. They must provide opportunities for offenders to address their offending at a personal level, and assist in the successful reintegration back into society".[5]

For most inmates, the corrections experience is in fact drastically the opposite. Whereas some local yokel might go into our corrections system ignorant to progressive criminal activity, they now have an ample amount of free time on their hands, compiled with a huge network of criminals from all sorts of disciplines in the criminal underworld.

A man or woman serving even a few years of time for a lighter crime now has access to the best schooling and training in criminal enterprising, all of which is paid for by our government.

Many of these green horns are absolutely and completely ill-equipped to cope with the cruelty of prison life. Some offenders are there due to mental illness, yet approximately 30% of prisons do not even provide any type of psychiatric care.[6]

The very nature of living in a prison environment can suck the life marrow out of the soul. As Elaine Bartless writes in her book on her own prison experiences, "prison living can be the worst sort of training for future employment. Not surprisingly, many inmates grow so used to being in an institution— of being told when to eat, when to sleep, when to go to the toilet—that they lose all of their ambition and initiative, precisely the qualities they will need to get a job once they are set free".[7]

She writes about the importance of being able to have a job while you are serving time in prison. Any type of job to get your mind off of the sheer boredom and monotony of prison life. She said that she was lucky to have been given a job in the prison, but that some inmates "want to work, yet there are not enough jobs to go around."

She shares her insights on the fact that an offender finishes their sentence and serves time, but returns back to the same original position with no job skills and the only glaring option of returning to criminal life as a source of generating a cash flow.

She adds, "even if a prisoner does land a job [in prison], there is no guarantee that he or she will possess marketable skills when released. Pushing a broom around a cell block or scooping food onto trays in the mess hall does not prepare one for anything more than minimum-wage work".[8]

Once again, we see the vicious cycle. We hold these men and women behind bars for a few years, and we hope that they hated it so much that they will never return. Yet, after losing a few years of their life behind prison walls, they are still back at square one with no opportunities for creating an honest living to support themselves and their loved ones. For those recently released from prison and in need of quick cash, the buying and selling of handguns is an option that is all too easy to fall into.

Bernard Harcourt writes, "handguns represent a commodity to be traded or sold for cash or drugs. Guns are their way of participating in our market economy." Harcourt quotes an offender who shares his story, "sell [guns] and party, and buy things, stereos, gold, I can help my family out, I can rent hotel rooms, buy all kinds of beer, and live the fast life".[9]

What we are saying is that we give ex-offenders next to nothing when released. We do not supply them with a new set of friends that are positive, inspiring and uplifting. We do not supply them with people who genuinely love them and care about them, and want them to do something good with their lives.

We do not provide them with skills that enable them to go out and find a job that pays more than minimum wage, or with the skills to start their own small business from scratch. In that vacuum, on the other side of the fence, they have countless voices of former friends who are luring them back to the old way of life.

Easy money, easy sex, easy drugs. It takes an exceedingly powerful force to counterbalance all of those overwhelming negative influences and insure that the recently released offender will continue to pursue good and wholesome undertakings, and do all they can do to avoid the negative influences that are calling them back to their former life.

Ex-offenders frequently have very few friends who serve as a positive influence or role model in their lives, and no doubt endure an endless gauntlet of negative peer pressure parading before them upon their return to the neighborhood after serving time. Even the most resolute and determined offender eventually feels the overwhelming pressures, inequitably balanced far more on the negative, than on the positive. A dozen old friends stopping by to pay a visit, enticing you back to the old way of life.

For many, those who are released from prison temporarily become the local folk hero in some neighborhoods. Something to talk about. Many first-time offenders lack the basic skills that would have otherwise enabled them to successfully integrate into society.

These basic skills include social skills that you and I take for granted, such as how to ask a woman out on a date, or how to make a new social friend. A longitudinal study was done of 411 boys who were born in working-class families.

The researchers followed these 411 boys throughout their lives, in hopes of uncovering patterns that might later serve to predict criminal behavior, and thereby teach us how to avoid it. D.P. Farrington found that those individuals among the 411 original boys chosen who became chronic repeat offenders had "showed symptoms of antisocial behavior quite early in life."

Many were identified as troublesome or dishonest in their early years in primary school, and, by age 10, had been identified as being impulsive, hyperactive and unpopular".[10]

By exposing weaker first time offenders to hardcore repeat offenders, we condition them and we train them. Not only in the art of better methods for engaging in the various sorts of crime they find appealing, but also how to become more sophisticated so as to evade the efforts of law enforcement authorities.

The only glimmer of hope that our society has in seeing any level of redemptive process at work within those concrete walls and bars is to possibly make the experience of serving time so unpleasant and so miserable that the offender reaches the point where he or she makes up their mind that they never want to return there ever again.

CHAPTER FOUR

*Let's Just Make It So Miserable, So They*
*Simply Do Not Want To Come Back*

Even with that mediocre and haphazard approach to the field of corrections, there are still a number of factors at play which eventually serve to both thwart and dilute such efforts. First of all, it is obvious that corrections administrators who might embrace such a philosophical approach have their hand restrained by laws which prohibit them from embarking on a reign of terror and bearing down too heavily upon the inmate population.

As a quick sidebar issue, it is interesting to note that some wardens do feel they have no choice but to pursue such a path regardless of the laws, citing the simple mathematical fact that in big city facilities there is often one corrections officer for every one hundred men.

These wardens point out the various obvious fact that it would not take too much of an effort for the inmate population to quickly organize themselves and over run the staff and seize control of the facility. We have indeed seen this done quite a number of times over the past several decades where an uprising among the inmate population broke out and many corrections officers were killed or severely injured in the riots. With such an argument, these wardens believe they have no other option but to create and instill an exceptionally high level of fear and intimidation in order to maintain social control over the greater numbers that they are paid to manage.

Back to our previous argument, the second point that dilutes the impact of the "create a miserable experience" approach is that for many among the inmate population, the transition from the outside world to the inside world of the corrections facilities does not carry the sting and culture shock that it does for others among the population. It is logically argued that many who come from crime ridden housing projects already experience the severe restraints of poverty, whereby they have very little to do other than hang out with no money to go anywhere. That can be easily coupled with the emotional intensity and constant threat of danger that go hand in hand in some of these more violent and poverty stricken projects. For some individuals, if they have no resources to obtain food, at least now they are assured of getting meals three times a day.

They might be meeting up with a number of friends from the neighborhood who have been imprisoned for several years. Some repeat offenders have confided during news interviews that life inside of the four walls for them is somewhat better than the meager and dreary existence they endured while living outside and back at the housing project. As bizarre as this confession might sound to some, you need only squirrel up your courage to go driving through some of these housing projects, and you will gain for yourself a very quick understanding of why such inmates might feel that way.

Now to summarize our point and counterpoint. We stated that the overall corrections system in the United States does very little towards affecting an experience whereby the offender is rehabilitated and returned to society. We pointed out that the only glimmer of hope we generally have is that the inmate might experience such an intensity of misery that they make a conscious decision to never again return to such a facility ever again. We then pointed out that for many among the inmate population, there is no such experience, and that the transition from civilian life to inmate life is a very minor change for them. Among some of the inmate population, the quality of life while incarcerated might even be an improvement over their previous lives when they roamed the streets freely.

C H A P T E R   F I V E

### *Why Doesn't Someone Do Something About All of This?*

Earlier we discussed the alarming statistics of this huge cog in the wheels of modern society, made the point that our design for the system of correcting our offenders is so overwhelmingly flawed that we fail 70% of the time. At least one-third of those convicted felons who serve time in our correctional facilities, are doomed to get arrested again within three years and return to be incarcerated once again. These already alarming statistics are significantly increased if we expand that time window of only three years, to a greater variable of five years, six years, and so on.

We also made the very valid point that in no other industry in our country would there be such a foolhardy tolerance of utter failure. We have employed this completely flawed philosophy of corrections for more than 200 years, willingly accepting its dismal track record of failure as the fruit of its malfunction continually eats away at our society like a massive cancer.

Why do we tolerate such failure? Have the powers that have so effectively numbed our minds with brainless reality television brought us to the point of feeling completely powerless to speak up and get involved? Does it have to reach the point where criminals are over-running local law enforcement to get to the point where everyday citizens find themselves motivated to start speaking up and drawing attention to problems that we should be working on fixing?

Despite two centuries of dreadful deficiency, we have not seen any concerted effort step forward to spearhead the great undertaking of revolutionizing and revitalizing our corrections system. A number of protests here and there, mostly centered on some inmate that support the claim that they have been wrongfully incarcerated. We've also had a number of grassroots efforts regarding politically heated topics such as the ethics of capital punishment, but never among them a grand proposal for implementing a massive countrywide overhaul of this metastatic corrections system. Never a light bearer pointing out its flaws and the overwhelming price paid by the rest of us who love being a member of a somewhat civilized society. Never one to boldly contrive a plan and ask for the green light to go forward and implement the massive changes to that out-of-date malformed monstrosity we mockingly refer to as the Federal Department of Corrections.

CHAPTER SIX

*Can't We Be The Best In The World?*

One can almost hear the well-rehearsed rhetoric of the seasoned politician, ranting some simple minded canned answer such as, "well, it's not a perfect system, but it is the best in the world."

Nothing could be further from the truth. Our corrections system is light years away from being the best in the world.

Let's take a look at our brothers and sisters across the pond, and examine some of the success rates of foreign prisons. How is it that the race of people we fled from some four hundred years ago, always seem to be serving as the sociological conscious of humankind. As if they have somehow stepped into the shoes of Jiminy Cricket and been deputized by a fairy to be Pinocchio's mentor, the Europeans always seem to be a light year or two ahead of us when it comes to sociological and humanitarian policies and beliefs.

Last century, when the world was aghast at our practice of kidnapping foreign citizens from their villages and huts and demanding that they give up their families to become our slaves, it was the Europeans who repeatedly voiced their angst at the brutality of our actions. "How can one man own another man," the Europeans loudly protested to other citizen countries throughout the globe. Over the decades, it has always been the Europeans who seemed to be trailblazers among the more evolved issues to be wrestled with in a truly civilized society. Should it be any surprise, then, when we discover that many European prisons hold a completely astounding recidivism rate as low as 15%?

How can we, who arrogantly (and falsely) pride ourselves as being "the world's only superpower" be content to blithely tolerate a 70% recidivism rate?

Why can we not get down from our self-imposed ivory towers of self-glorification and at least pretend to be interested in learning how the Europeans are able to achieve such an amazing feat. Let's consider going back to the earlier purpose of prisons in the United States, which was to provide a vehicle for correcting those who have lost their way and fallen prey to a criminal mentality. That is, after all, how we came up with the universally adopted term of "Department of Corrections", isn't it? Perhaps a more accurate term if we chose something new today might be "Department of Criminal Warehousing". Better yet, "Department of Continuing Criminal Education".

Let's take a look at where we stand with our Department of Corrections. Figure 6.1 Rate of Incarceration, by Country,[11] shows that the United States has a substantially higher percentage of its citizens living in prison than all other countries.[12] We have the highest rate of incarceration, more than any country in the world.

### Rate of Incarceration in Selected Nations

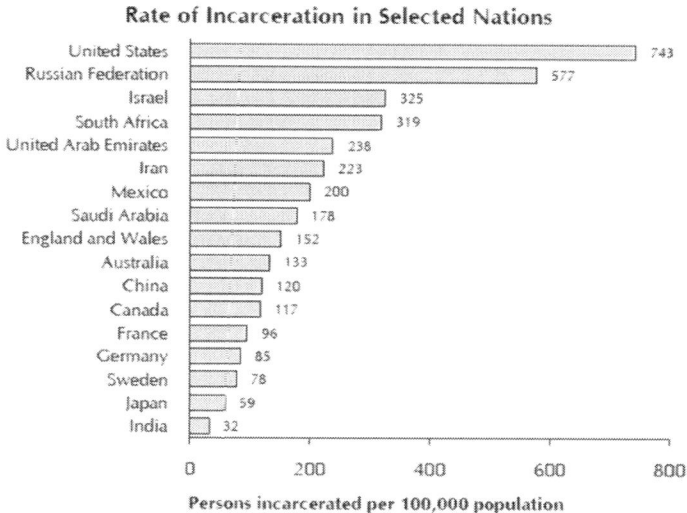

| Country | Persons incarcerated per 100,000 population |
|---|---|
| United States | 743 |
| Russian Federation | 577 |
| Israel | 325 |
| South Africa | 319 |
| United Arab Emirates | 238 |
| Iran | 223 |
| Mexico | 200 |
| Saudi Arabia | 178 |
| England and Wales | 152 |
| Australia | 133 |
| China | 120 |
| Canada | 117 |
| France | 96 |
| Germany | 85 |
| Sweden | 78 |
| Japan | 59 |
| India | 32 |

Persons incarcerated per 100,000 population

Figure 6-1 Rate of Incarceration, by Country

I know there are many people involved with prison reform who take a strong issue on that fact alone, and they feel that perhaps our criminal justice system sentences people to prison for crimes that they should not have to serve time for, such as nonviolent crimes. I honestly do not take that stand at all. What I am concerned about, and the reason I wrote this book, is the simple fact that our current Department of Corrections system makes these people worse. It clearly does not serve as a deterrent to future crime. What good is it to sentence people to prison if they only come back home angrier, more violent, and more inclined to commit more crimes. We are victimizing ourselves without even realizing what we are doing.

When I first learned that our country has the highest incarceration rate in the world, I was quite a bit surprised. I can think of several countries off the top of my head that probably would deserve that status more than our country does, don't you agree? If a friend were to invite us on a trip abroad traveling to several other countries for a month or two, there are a number of countries that come to mind where we might say to our friend, "no, I wouldn't want to go to that country, because they are so full of crime and violent criminals."

Looking down the list of these other countries on the chart, wouldn't you have to agree that we seem to feel that our own country is relatively safe versus quite a number of those other countries on the list? I know that's what my reaction is every time I look on that list. One country is known for kidnapping and demanding a hefty ransom from family members, another known for robberies, another is known for drug cartels, and so on.

Another startling statistic that took me by surprise is how our rate of incarceration of Americans sharply increased during the last 40 years. In Figure 6.2

Incarcerated Americans 1920-2014,[13] we see that in 1980 and 1990, the rates of incarceration suddenly began to shoot up. Some say it is because the country started adopting a "tough on crime" stance, but I feel that as a whole our country has always been tough on crime. The chart shows incarceration rates starting from the 1920s and 1930s, and when I think of that era, the first historical figure is Elliott Ness and his Untouchables fighting underworld crime that exploded during The Prohibition. Advocates of that theory are suggesting that we had been relatively soft on crime from the 1920s through the 1970s, and then suddenly we became tough on crime. No, I honestly do not see this as a driving force behind the dramatic change.

Another very good argument would be that this is when the nation decided to really get tough on illegal drugs. The chart does seem to coincide with the explosion of cocaine and other narcotics. That's certainly a good argument worth looking into.

My own opinion would be more inclined to speculate more along the lines that this might be about the time that we started switching from being a country that seeks to rehabilitate our inmate population, and instead becoming one that simply seeks to sweep the problem under the rug and temporarily warehouse our criminal offenders. We went from trying to turn their lives around so that they stop preying upon us, to just taking them off the streets for a while and cross our fingers that they decide not to ever go back prison. Our nation has paid a huge price for that change in policy, a price we often refuse to see.

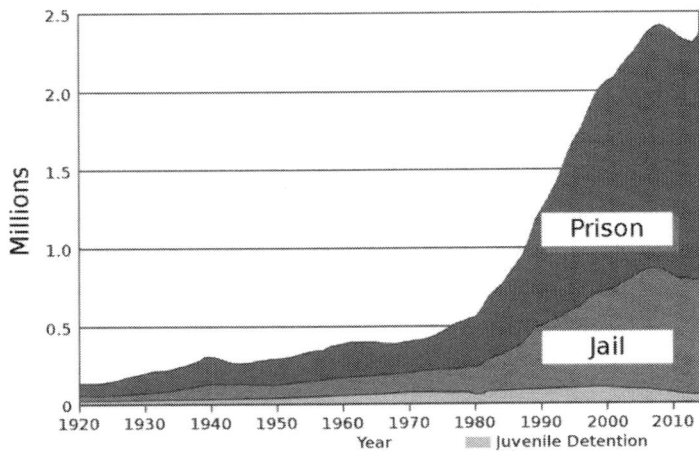

Figure 6.2 Incarcerated Americans 1920-2014

C H A P T E R   S E V E N

## *Is It Better to Strip or To Retain Human Dignity?*

Do the Europeans enjoy such success because they have removed the legal constraints we have here in the United States, whereby our laws prohibit us from employing methodologies that would be considered cruel and unusual punishment? No, not at all. Quite the opposite. The Europeans actually take the title of "Department of Corrections" seriously, and they endeavor to do just that. Their honest and true objective is to correct and rehabilitate each and every man and woman that sets foot inside their walls of concrete and iron bars. It is their highest objective to re-integrate those people into society, and creating within each individual the desire to become a willing and happy participant in the roles that society can offer, as well as to reap its benefits and rewards.

They do not believe in stripping a human being of their dignity in order to break them down and attempt to reform them. No, they fully realize that if you pit yourself in an adversarial relationship against the incarcerated, those inmates will most likely respond in kind, and similarly pit themselves against the system as well. It becomes a vicious cycle that inevitably results in lose-lose scenarios. For example, they do not restrict their felons of the right to vote. In fact, wardens encourage the inmates to vote for candidates running for office, and they do all they can to accommodate the electoral process for those men and women who are serving time behind their walls.

Another example of retaining human dignity examines our own practice of sending convicted felons to institutions that might be hundreds or thousands of miles away from families. Here in our barbaric and flawed philosophy, we seem to believe this cuts off any social support that the inmate might enjoy, resulting in an inmate that is more malleable, and more easily controlled. Again, an incredibly stupid approach. In Europe, they know this does not work and they employ quite the opposite approach. They see the family members as extensions and ambassadors of the corrections system, and leverage the power of caring family members to urge and persuade that incarcerated man or woman to give up their criminal ways, and to instead embrace the more fulfilling aspects of wholesome living be repriotizing family life.

By putting our loved ones before ourselves, even the coldest of human hearts will soon enjoy a wellspring of good will and compassion for others springing forth. It is a powerful tool of personal rehabilitation that can be easily utilized by any skillful or knowledgeable corrections specialist or rehabilitation counselor seeking to re-integrate an offender back into society.[14]

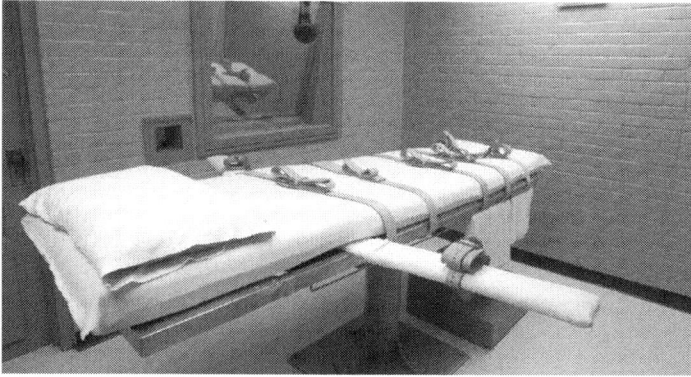

CHAPTER EIGHT

Does the Death Penalty Really Help
Reduce Any Crime At All?

While examining the need for prison reform, let's take
a look at a few related topics that may or may not impact
the recidivism rate, and the rehabilitation of our criminal
offenders. For example, the death penalty. Despite
volumes of evidence to the contrary, there are still many
people in our nation that believe that the implementation
of the death penalty serves to reduce crime. As if some
gang banger were to suddenly stop his fit of murderous
range, piously ponder and reflect, and suddenly come to
the thunderbolt revolution of "no, I better not stab this guy
here, or I might get arrested and then be executed by lethal
injection." No, that certainly does not happen.

In fact, I was quite surprised to learn that in many of
the counties and cities where execution by lethal injection
is legal, and the criminal justice system in those locations
continues to kill convicts with a haphazard belief that by

killing murderers, we will teach others in society that it is wrong to kill people, those areas of the country often have a much higher crime rate than the areas which do not kill their hardcore convicted murderers. What an irony! The Wall Street Journal recently carried an article reporting that the Supreme Court has given their official stand and legal opinion that the lethal injection does qualify as a cruel and unusual punishment in the execution of convicted killers. They believe that drug injections to execute defendants sentenced to death causes undue pain and suffering upon the criminal. Some states do agree with this legal position, and executions by lethal injections have been outlawed in several states, including Maryland, North Carolina and Ohio.

When our Founding Fathers constructed their own system of jurisprudence, they wove in the beliefs of mercy upon the accused. They firmly believed in a new system whereby it is better that a few guilty should go free, rather than one innocent man be imprisoned. In our day, however, it seems quite the opposite. There have been quite a number of men who have been executed, and their innocence of the crime they were charged with was later revealed based on new evidence. Sadly, they were only exonerated posthumously.

A study published in the Stanford Law Review cited that since the year 1900, there were more than twenty-three such people who were put to death and wrongfully executed.[15] Of the men and women currently sentenced to death row, more than one-hundred such offenders have been found innocent and subsequently released based on cutting edge DNA investigation proving them innocent of the crimes upon which they were accused and sentenced.[16]

Sharp sheds some further light on wrongful convictions, "all cases do not present the opportunity for [DNA] testing. Many persons on death row are sentenced based on less conclusive evidence, [such as] eyewitness testimony, false confessions, jailhouse informants and junk science are all frequent sources of error".[17]

Another argument mentioned in this article of those who lobby their opinions that our Federal government should cease using lethal injections state that sometimes a prison will select personnel to perform the injection that are not fully medically qualified. As a result, there have indeed been instances where the execution experienced some setbacks and the procedure was drawn out longer than it should have taken to terminate the individual. Additionally, there have been a few circumstances where the lethal injection process failed, and the convict actually survived the lethal injection of these heavily toxic chemicals and lived through the procedure.

One legal dispute that has gone back and forth was whether or not one of the three drugs in the cocktail, the anesthetic thiopental sodium, was really doing its job sufficiently enough in driving the convict into a detached state of mind where they no longer felt any pain. They put forth the question as to whether the sentenced defendant is truly fully unconsciousness before the second and third drugs that actually cause the body to die are administered, or whether the inmate can feel the pain of these secondary injections as they enter the body and subdue it. Their opinion is that if the inmate is still even partially conscious, the pain experienced is exceptionally excruciating.

Amidst the various legal issues that are swirling about in this article, there is the somewhat surprising news story that the drugs that have been warehoused for employing death by lethal execution are approaching the end of their shelf life and are expiring. To complicate things further, the article indicates there is a shortage of the supply of drugs used in creating the cocktail of death injected into the veins of the doomed aggressor.

You can see from this chart in Figure 8.1 Death
Penalty vs. Non-Death Penalty States,[18] that the threat of
the death penalty has absolutely no impact on reducing
crime, at least for murders. In fact, the chart indicates that
the states that do have a death penalty also have a higher
murder rate.

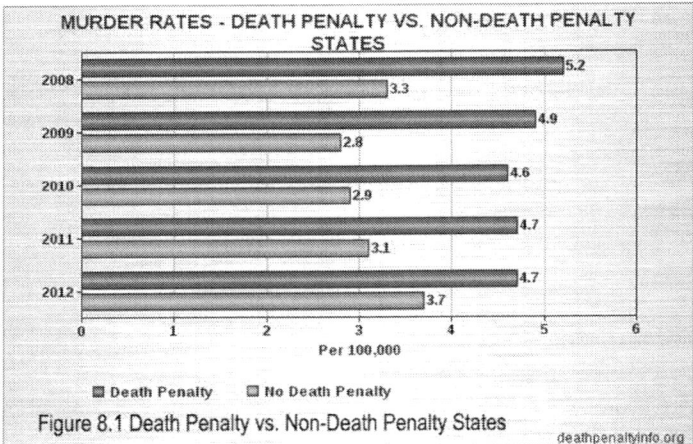

Figure 8.1 Death Penalty vs. Non-Death Penalty States

Those who advocate for the death penalty sometimes
will theorize that the murder rates are somehow linked to
various locations around the country and that this is
somehow muddying the waters regarding whether or not
the death penalty really is or is not a deterrent for crimes
such as murder.

They will say that murders are more commonplace in
those states on the East coast or the West coast, compared
to those in the mid-west. To address that concern, we can
look at states that have a death penalty and identify a
neighboring state that does not have a death penalty.

That potential argument does not hold up under closer
scrutiny. Let's take a look at Figure 8.2 where we compare
the murder rate of states with the death penalty and that of

a neighboring state without the death penalty. Missouri, Connecticut, Illinois, and Virginia are four states that do have a death penalty.

As predicted based on what we learned earlier, each of those states also have a high murder rate. If we look at a state neighboring Missouri, that does not have the death penalty, such as Iowa, we see their murder rate is much lower.

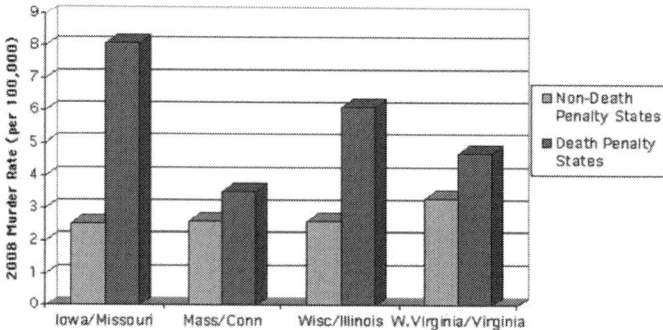

Figure 8.2 Comparing Neighboring States

The same exact situation holds true for the remaining three states. Massachusetts does not have the death penalty, yet it is a neighbor to Connecticut and the murder rate is higher in Connecticut.

The same thing happens with Wisconsin and Illinois, where the murder rate is much lower in Wisconsin and they do not have the death penalty. Finally we look at West Virginia and Virginia, with West Virginia not having the death penalty and yet their murder rate is lower than Virginia, which does have the death penalty.

Should we abolish the death penalty? We are not necessarily saying that. We are just pointing out that the death penalty is not a deterrent to crime as is commonly believed.

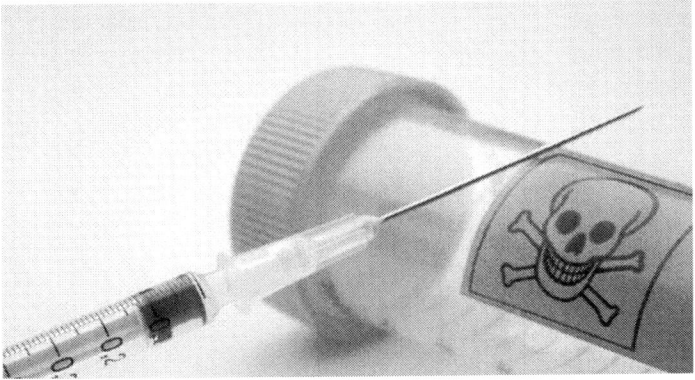

C H A P T E R   N I N E

*Identifying the Chemicals*
*Within the Lethal Injections*

In researching these and other aspects of the death penalty, it was surprising to learn that one of the other components of the lethal injection is a drug that paralyzes the muscles of the felon awaiting their final seconds of life.[19] There are three different types of drugs that are in the compound used for lethal injections.[20] The first drug is a barbiturate that causes the convict to be rendered unconscious. The next drug is the paralytic that makes the skeletal muscles become completely immobilized. Third, potassium chloride is used to cause the heart to stop beating.

If you have ever had surgery where an anesthesiologist was involved, you know that the injected substance (some of these used in such surgeries are midazolam, propofol, diazepam, diphenhydramine, promethazine, meperidine, and fentanyl) that knocks you out is very effective. Why, then, the need to completely paralyze the muscles of the felon? To the astute reader, it immediately seems that something is afoot regarding this component of the elixir of expiration.

CHAPTER TEN

*Why Are There Mixed Messages from the Proponents?*

It's one thing if they told us up front and were honest about saying that lethal injections in prison executions is painful. Fine. But they don't. They lie and say it is not painful. Hmmm... Okay, if it is not painful, I do have some questions.

You know, as a child I loved watching the old Lone Ranger television series. I can remember one actor saying, "white man speak with forked tongue" as the wise old chief recognized the signs of deceit and deception in his dealings with the dominant culture.

To this writer, the addition of a pharmaceutical grade paralytic would seem to raise a red flag. Someone is speaking with a forked tongue. My question is this. Why would you need to paralyze the inmate if the death dealing injections were pain free as they claim? This would certainly appear to endorse and confirm the argument of the lobbyists against the death penalty that those being subject to death by injection are indeed experiencing extreme physical torment and pain. Otherwise, what other possible reason could there be to include such a pharmaceutical in the concoction?

Logic would seem to dictate that in the early days of experimenting with execution by lethal injection, the doctors of death probably observed that the squeamish general public sitting in the audience were recoiling in horror as they watched their doomed prisoner writhing in pain and agony. Hence, they cooked up the scheme of infiltrating the broth for the banished with the necessary component that would completely paralyze the individual,[21] thereby making it nearly impossible for the general laymen to discern the extreme physical pain the doomed man was experiencing as his nerve endings burned with fire in the last remaining minute or two of life in this world.

There are more than 3,200 inmates that have been sentenced to death by the death penalty. The U.S. Department of Justice also tells us that there has been a very sharp increase in the number of prisoners sentenced to death.

Those who advocate for the abolishment of the death penalty claim that the majority are poor, uneducated, and black. The chart[22] in Figure 10.1 shows us that the rate of prisoners being sentenced to death in America has been sharply escalating since

1981. (Keep in mind that the death penalty was
reinstated by the Supreme Court in 1976.)

    We can see from this chart a breakdown by race.
We note that more than half of those individuals that
are under the sentence of death have been Caucasian,
and the second highest ranking in race is African-
American.

**Race of those under sentence of death**

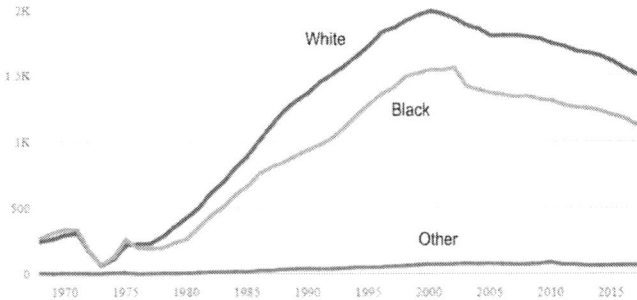

Figure 10.1 Inmates on Death Row by Race, 1970 - 2015

    I know, you might be thinking that sometimes it
seems like I am presenting arguments on both sides of the
fence, right? Well, that's part of the problem and that's
part of why you do not see any movement on either side
for years and years. That's why a stalemate on these issues
can literally last for decades. It's because both sides make
up things and blur the facts. Like my father used to say, "if
you catch someone lying about one fact, you have to start
wondering what else might they be lying about."

CHAPTER ELEVEN

*Am I My Brother's Keeper?*

In his 1911 book "The House of the Dead: Prison Life in Siberia", Fyodor Dostoyevsky wrote, "the degree of civilization in a society can be judged by entering their prisons." Similarly, Winston Churchill said, "you can judge a society by the way it treats its prisoners."

Among the world's overall population, the total number of citizens in our country is only 5%. Yet, among the overall world's population of people currently serving time in prison, our country has 25% of the world's inmate population incarcerated here in American prisons. Among the leading countries of the world, the United States has the highest rate per capita of incarceration of its citizens.

We arrest more than 14 million of our citizens every year.[23] This undeniably screams out that something is very wrong with our system, and our society. So, why don't we start working to fix it? Setting aside the ethical and moral imperative to do the right thing, we cannot ignore the landfill of cash and tax dollars we would save if we could significantly reduce our recidivism rates.

How much money would we save? Let's just take a rough guess. Approximately 2.3 million people are incarcerated in the United States on any given day. The United States Bureau of Prisons states that the average annual cost for housing an inmate for one year in a federal prison is approximately $28,000 per inmate. Another source, the Vera Institute of Justice, states the average cost for housing an inmate ranges from $31,000 to as much as $60,000 in some states. Costs will vary depending on whether the inmate is in a federal, state, or county prison. So let's pick a number and go for around $26,000 per year. If we multiply that $26k by the 2.3 million that are incarcerated, we have an estimated $59.8 billion spent every year to house our prison population.

We have already said that the average recidivism rate in the United States is around 77%, so let's multiply the $59.8 billion by 77%. That would suggest we are spending $46 billion just on recidivism! Let's use our imagination and say that if we magically wiped out recidivism completely (which is obviously unrealistic), that is $46 billion that we could invest elsewhere in our infrastructure. How about better housing, better education, better schools, lower costs for attending state college, etc. There are a hundred different things we could come up with that we could invest that $46 billion into, don't you agree?

We surely cannot ignore the fact that there is a very long list of other sociological endeavors that we could otherwise be investing our financial wealth and resources into. During a tough economic downward spiral, where many municipal and state governments are forced to make ugly budget cuts to continue floating, it sure would be very welcome news to anticipate a sudden influx of tax dollars that we know would be saved if we were to fix our corrections machinery and reduce recidivism.

I believe that we truly have no other option but to recognize the simple fact that the mere existence of men and women who commit violent crime are symptoms that we have a malfunctioning society. Ultimately, therefore, we as a society do shoulder some of the weight of responsibility of these men and women who have committed crimes deemed worthy of execution.

If we were to view such ills of society in the context of observing a gasoline engine that is sputtering and coughing up blue smoke, we would know that the engine needs to be adjusted and fine-tuned so that its chugging can be smoothed out and the engine can then run smoothly.

Similarly, the rising numbers of men and women incarcerated each year are likewise symptomatic that there are undercurrents in our way of life that are leaving countless numbers of people to come to that crossroads in life where they begin to perceive a life of crime as their only available alternative to enjoying a comfortable standard of living.

CHAPTER TWELVE

## *Looking to the Future*

No doubt the debate over capital punishment will go on and on throughout the future, with neither side coming to the point where they see eye to eye or reach a middle ground. We also see that our society has countless problems that are festering due to both our neglect, and also prioritizing on other areas such as extreme focus on military spending. By our deliberate neglect, we are creating setbacks that force millions of Americans down below the poverty level where day to day survival can be overwhelming.

While more than 40% of our populace lives in poverty, we still flood our television airwaves with high impact videos of people who live in large houses, drive beautiful, expensive cars and live a lifestyle far beyond their reach. It is inevitable that such incongruence explodes like a volcano and many struggle with emotions of anger and rage. Evidence of this is the fact that our country has one of the highest rates of imprisonment, as well as an astronomical rate of recidivism.

Ultimately I believe that we as a society do indeed bear responsibility of our fellow Americans, and that we are indeed our brother's keeper. In the new paradigm of "Social Imagination", we should be viewing others who are in pain as if we ourselves are in pain. When those who commit horrendous crimes are given the death sentence, it reflects upon the rest of us and the neglect that we have allowed to continue which creates the circumstances that push people into a life of crime. Should we then be soft on crime? No, definitely not. But I do believe we need to fix our corrections system so that it stops being a revolving door.

Since I have been the victim of violent attacks ("muggings") several times, I know what it can feel like and how it can eat away at you for months.

What would it take to reduce recidivism in America and thereby reduce the amount of crimes our citizens fall victim to each year? We have all heard that for the price of warehousing an individual in prison for five years, you could purchase a Harvard education for them. With tuition at Harvard costing $47,730 per year, that's probably very close to being true and it is something worth thinking about.

One challenge that inmates face when they are released is that they do not have much to look forward to if there isn't a supportive family dedicated to helping them. Finding work is going to be hard with a criminal record. You are looking at accepting a minimum wage job that you cannot really support yourself with.

Let's say you are released from prison and are determined to never go back. You want to better yourself and go to college. It is hard to get a college education if you do not have a family helping you. Many younger students in the age bracket of 18 to 22 have a hard time paying for tuition, even at a community college. Students at that age are often unable to apply for loans until they are age 25. They have to find other alternatives, or try to work their way through way through school, which is

often too much for many students. (It was too much for
me, I remember. I did not have the stamina for it.)
Shouldn't we make it easier for students to get a college
education if they really wanted to?

As the chart in Figure 12.1 shows, one of the most
successful experiences an inmate can have while locked
up is to engage in an educational program. For many
inmates in the past, they shared that the first time that they
had an experience of someone they looked up to believing
in them was when they enrolled in a class of some kind
within the confines of the prison walls. You may not know
it, but back in 1994 President Clinton signed legislation
that removed the funding for prison inmates to enroll in
educational programs while they were in prison. The 1994
Omnibus Crime Bill brought a number of changes to the
criminal justice system, to include the removal of Pell
Grants for the education of inmates. This included GED
programs, remedial high school classes, and courses for
college credit.

A very simple reduction in recidivism can be found
simply in teaching prisons a vocation so that they could
find decent work paying a decent wage when they leave
the correction system. In the past an inmate could learn
skills such as plumbing, welding, electrical wiring and
such. Those opportunities are no longer. There are a small
handful of prisons that have been fortunate to have an
outside school raise their own funds in order to conduct
college level courses in a few jails and prisons. Some even
grant college credit for their coursework. This is a
wonderful incentive for the inmate to seek to continue
their college education after being released.

We see how the changes that President Clinton made
and the removal of educational programs while
incarcerated have snowballed. The American prison
population has exploded with runaway recidivism. During
the Clinton years, the prison population nearly doubled

from 600,000 living behind bars to 1.2 million. Those numbers have continued growing. It is not too difficult to imagine the rates of recidivism one day escalating to as much as 85% to 90% if we don't start thinking outside of the box and changing how we do things. Along with that, we know that the costs of prisons have continued rising. It is a vicious cycle that is quite clearly out of control.

**Inmate Education Among the Most Effective Programs At Reducing Recidivism**

*Percentage Reduction in Recidivism (2006 National Data)*

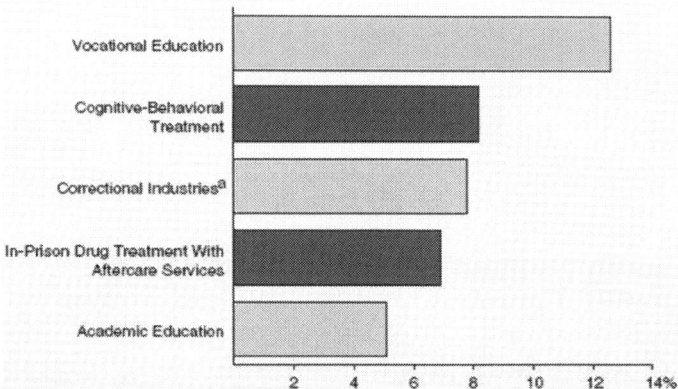

Source: Washington State Institute for Public Policy.
[a] In some cases, these programs incorporate vocational education.

Figure 12.1 Programs That Reduce Recidivism

Are there forces that are blocking the corrections system from being improved? Yes, most definitely! Many want to keep things just as they are, despite the huge expense on tax-payers and the problems caused by repeat offenders who prey upon society.

Back before 1980, there was no such thing as private prisons. They gained a foothold and got the concept passed in legislature by promising how much more effective they would be. Now among inmates, the private prisons are generally considered to be the worst situation an inmate can find themselves in. The healthcare is worse, the security is worse, the opportunities for personal development are worse, the violence of fighting among inmates is worse.

If you think about it, a good argument could be made that there is a financial incentive to keep things just as they are. There are profits generated by the fact that recidivism is so high in this country.

If the Europeans can figure out how to make the corrections system actually do what it is supposed to do, meaning to rehabilitate prisoners, why can't the United States?

Another area that needs to be worked on is the creation of more re-entry programs to help an ex-offender when they are released. For many inmates, it is common that the family has grown tired of their many dramas and has cut them off. They receive very little contact from friends or loved ones. When they are released, many of them do not have any type of re-entry program to help them find housing, help them find a job, and help them get reacquainted with day to day living. Who comes looking for them? Most often it is the same crew that got them on the wrong path to begin with.

Finding a way to build up more re-entry programs can make a huge difference in reducing and preventing recidivism. Sometimes just a friendly face who wants to offer a helping hand can be enough to tip the odds in their favor if they really want to make a difference and never go back.

Even simple things like how to prepare for a job interview, how to handle yourself during the interview process, how to fill out a job application, how to dress appropriately for a job interview. These are all some basic skills that you and I might take for granted but that are foreign to many who have served time behind bars.

I'm thinking of a young ex-offender who had a bad streak of luck and wound up homeless living in his truck in a campground. I somehow managed to interest him in becoming a student in the local community college. He had served a few years behind bars and then went to a vo-tech school to become a welder. Apparently that didn't work out and he did not have a steady job.

After he agreed to give the local community college a try, I went with him to fill out the applications and financial aid paperwork. I could see it was all a bit overwhelming for him, so I made a point of trying to ease his discomfort and awkward feelings by telling him some of my favorite jokes and tried to keep him laughing. I can still vividly remember standing at the Registrar's desk and he asked, "When will I know if I am accepted into this community college or not?" The woman looked at me, then back at him, and smiled when she said, "Oh, you are accepted right now." He looked at me with a big grin. He totally lit up with joy.

Next they took his photograph and gave him his college identification card. He was so proud of that. That college identification card seems to be something so small and seemingly insignificant for most college students, but to him it was a badge of honor. I would catch him looking at that college identification card here and there, as if staring in disbelief that he was actually a college student.

I found out that he needed money up front while waiting on his financial aid package to come through. I loaned him the $800 and explained very carefully that I needed this money back the day that his loans came through. It took about five weeks. When the financial aid package came through, he repaid me in full without any problems at all.

I carefully and slowly showed him basic study skills. I did my best to transfer some enthusiasm from me to him and then paint a picture in his mind's eye of what it would be like when he finished his first semester. I knew that within two to three weeks, the excitement would wear off and it would start to become a grind. I desperately wanted to see him succeed and do well.

Most students in public school are never given any official training and instruction on how to study effectively. We spent a lot of time going over what I felt are the basic skills in studying in a strategic manner. I had developed a system for studying that worked quite reliably and helped me to get straight A's. I showed him how I go about absorbing everything in our textbooks to score high in the exams. I enrolled in two of the same classes he was in so that he would have some peer support.

Much to my amazement and delight, it all clicked and fell into place for him! He did very well that first semester. Within weeks he looked and behaved like a new man. It was one of the most incredible transformations that I have been blessed to witness first-hand. He was absolutely thrilled at being able to achieve A's and B's his first semester in college. He enrolled for the second semester and did well on his own. I was so very proud of him.

Working with a homeless ex-offender and helping him to turn his life around was one of the most rewarding experiences I have ever had the privilege to enjoy in this world. You cannot begin to imagine the depth of joy that can be experienced when you play a role in transforming the life of a person who has gone through one overwhelming setback after another. He was a person who had disappointed many others and was wrestling with self-loathing and self-contempt.

By succeeding in college and getting A's and B's that first semester, it gave him something real to point at and buoyed his self-esteem in ways that could not have been accomplished in any other manner. It was something real and tangible that could never be taken away from him.

I'm reminded of the Star Thrower story, first published in 1969 by Loren Eiseley. The story has been adapted by inspirational speakers along the lines of a man walking the beach early in the morning, throwing starfish back into the sea. An onlooker comments about how futile it is trying to save all the starfish, that it is an impossible task and how he cannot possibly save them all. He responds back, "I may not be able to save them all, but I can certainly save this one starfish."

Prison reform work is very much the same way. It is too daunting a task to think we can fix the system in a meaningful way, but we can certainly get involved in doing one-on-one volunteer work in a local county jail or prison. You can become a Star Thrower. You can join a prison literacy program and learn how to teach inmates how to read and write. You can teach basic job interview skills. You can share some of the things you enjoy about life and stir up an interest in personal development, goal setting and preparing for a better future upon release.

Just as a series of events fell into place for the homeless ex-offender that enabled him to transform his life, perhaps one day we might see a series of events fall into place where our corrections system can be fixed and recidivism reduced to a mere five percent. Perhaps one day we can see an overall philosophy of corrections become one where the focus is on rehabilitating the offender and preparing them for re-entry into a life full of meaning and purpose.

# Notes

[1] "Direct Expenditure by Criminal Justice Function, 1982-2006," in *Expenditure Facts at a Glance*, U.S. Department of Justice, Office of Justice Programs, Bureau of Justice Statistics, 18 Dec 2008.

[2] "Bureau of Justice Statistics (BJS) - Recidivism of Prisoners Released in 30 States in 2005: Patterns from 2005 to 2010 - Update," Bureau of Justice Statistics (BJS), accessed July 29, 2020, https://www.bjs.gov/index.cfm?ty=pbdetail&iid=4986.

[3] Noah Berlatsky, Imprisonment (Farmington Hills: Greenhaven Press, 2010), 23.

[4] John D. Bessler, *Kiss of Death: America's Love Affair with the Death Penalty* (Boston: Northeastern University Press, 2003), xvii.

[5] Noah Berlatsky, *Imprisonment* (Farmington Hills: Greenhaven Press, 2010), 33.

[6] American Correctional Association, *The Female Offender; What Does the Future Hold*, Washington, D.C.: St. Mary's Press, 1990.

[7] Jennifer Gonnerman, *Life on the Outside: The Prison Odyssey of Elaine Bartlett* (London: Macmillan, 2005), 192.

[8] Jennifer Gonnerman, *Life on the Outside: The Prison Odyssey of Elaine Bartlett* (London: Macmillan, 2005), 192.

[9] Bernard E. Harcourt, *Guns, Crime, and Punishment in America* (New York: NYU Press, 2003), 87.

[10] Peter B. Ainsworth, *Offender Profiling and Crime Analysis* (Portland: Willan Publishing, 2001), 32.

[11] King's College of London, International Centre for Prison Studies, "Rate of Incarceration, By Country," King's College of London, accessed April, 2011, http://www.kcl.ac.uk./depsta/law/research/icps/worldb rief/.

[12] Rate of Incarceration, By Country, *World Prison Brief*, King's College of London, International Centre for Prison Studies. http://www.kcl.ac.uk./depsta/law/research/icps/worldb rief/

[13] Incarcerated Americans 1920-2014, U.S. Bureau of Justice Statistics Bulletin, NCJ 219416.

[14] Barbara H. Zaitzow, *Women in Prison, Gender and Social Control*, (Colorado: Lynne Rienner Publishers, 2003), 129.

[15] John D. Bessler, *Kiss of Death: America's Love Affair with the Death Penalty*, (Ann Arbor: Northeastern University Press, 2003), 73.

[16] Bessler, *Kiss of Death*, 74.

[17] Susan F. Sharp, *Hidden Victims, The Effects Of The Death Penalty On Families Of The Accused*, (Piscataway: Rutgers University Press, 2005), 111.

[18] Raymond Bonner and Ford Fessenden, "Absence Of Executions: States With No Death Penalty Share Lower Homicide Rates," *New York Times*, September 22, 2000.

[19] "The Death Penalty Is Dying," The Province, May 2001.

[20] Larry Petrash, "Lethal Injection, Firing Squad Raise Ethical Questions," Times Record News, June 20, 2010.

[21] Human Rights Watch, "So Long as They Die: Lethal Injections in the United States," www.HRW.org, last modified April 2006, https://www.hrw.org/reports/2006/us0406/.

[22] Bureau of Justice Statistics (BJS), "The Death Penalty in the US: What the Data Says," Capital Punishment and Correctional Population Data Tables, https://usafacts.org/articles/death-penalty-us-what-data-says/#race-of-those-under-sentence-of-death.

[23] Kim Masters Evans, *Crime, Prisons, and Jails* (Detroit: Gale Cengage Learning, 2010), 6.

# Can I Ask For Your Help?

If you found this book interesting, informative, or insightful, would you be kind enough to help me by please posting a brief little review on Amazon?

I read all comments and use your feedback and insights to guide me in writing future books and educational resources.

Writing a book often takes several hundred hours. Posting a book review helps budding writers like me to continue doing what we love most, which is using the written word to help other people and to make a strong positive impact where we can.

## Visit Here To Leave An Amazon Review
### www.ricksaldan.com/review-cc

*Your support is greatly appreciated!*

## Book covers by Rick Saldan

- HOW TO GO FROM TIMID SPEAKER TO AWARD WINNING SPEAKER — RICK SALDAN
- HOW TO GET FREEDOM FROM FEAR FOREVER — RICK SALDAN
- CONQUERING STRESS — RICK SALDAN
- SELF-ESTEEM DETERMINES OUR DESTINY — RICK SALDAN
- HOW TO GET STRAIGHT A'S — RICK SALDAN
- HOW TO BECOME A BOUNCE BACK PERSON — RICK SALDAN
- THE HEALING POWER OF LAUGHTER — RICK SALDAN
- FIND A MENTOR, BE A MENTOR — RICK SALDAN
- GET PLUGGED IN & POWERED UP! — RICK SALDAN
- Breaking Free of the Matrix — RICK SALDAN
- USING THEATRICAL STAGE MAGIC TO ASSESS COGNITIVE DEVELOPMENT — RICK SALDAN
- MOTIVATIONAL MAGIC SECRETS FOR STAYING MOTIVATED IN TOUGH TIMES — RICK SALDAN
- Confronting Racial Hatred With Classic Literature — by Rick Saldan
- LUPUS: How I Conquered Thriving After Doctors Say You Have Five Years Left To Live — RICK SALDAN
- Excelling With Excel Formulas — Rick Saldan
- COLD WAR ESSAYS OR SOCIETAL BREAKDOWN — by Rick Saldan

To view more of Rick's other writings,
visit his author page on Amazon:
www.amazon.com/author/ricksaldan

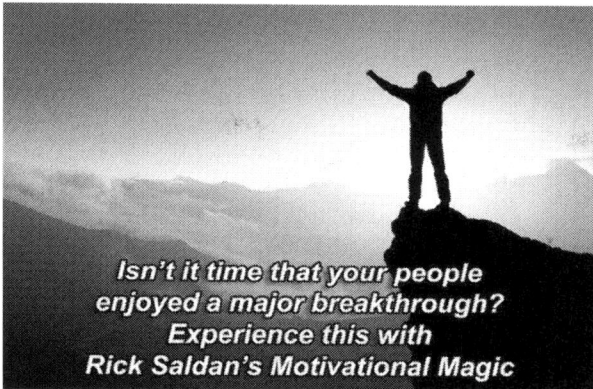

Isn't it time that your people enjoyed a major breakthrough? Experience this with Rick Saldan's Motivational Magic

### *Rick Wants to Help You and Your People!*

Rick has spoken to many audiences around the United States bringing an energizing message of inspiration. He loves to help people find their hidden gifts and strengths, and shows them how to activate them. Rick teaches people how to not only face their adversities and fears, but to allow difficulties to propel them further than they could go otherwise. He shows people how setbacks become stepping stones to something greater. Rick has countless true life examples of harsh adversities that were funneled and leveraged to help him grow. Your people will be inspired to do the same, and will no longer be held back from living and working to their fullest potential.

Rick's primary keynote message, "Secrets for Accomplishing the Impossible" is a high energy and fast paced presentation that is guaranteed to energize and keep your people on the edge of their seats. This is a powerful motivational event that your people will talk about for months to come. If you want your next special event to be truly spectacular, you'll want to invite Rick out to make your day more magical and exciting. You'll find Rick's

Motivational Magic to be one of the most uniquely creative and inspiring programs available.

Rick impacts your audience with powerful visual effects, followed by content rich educational sessions, astounding true life inspiring stories and motivational messages. All carefully designed and crafted to create an atmosphere that helps your people break through the barriers holding them back from their greatest accomplishments. The combined impact carries an intense emotional surge that creates the desire to take action.

Why is this important? Rick says, "I have been to countless seminars and conferences over the years. Within 3 days, participants have forgotten 90% of what they were taught. By creating an emotional surge, what you are teaching becomes imprinted in their minds. The rate of retention and application now increases dramatically! Participants become committed to taking action that will have impact." Your conference participants will say, "Rick was one of the best speakers we have ever had."

To hire Rick Saldan for your special event, visit his website at: **www.MotivationalMagic.com**

Imagine smashing through the barriers holding you back! Experience this with Rick Saldan's Motivational Magic

Made in the USA
Coppell, TX
07 September 2020